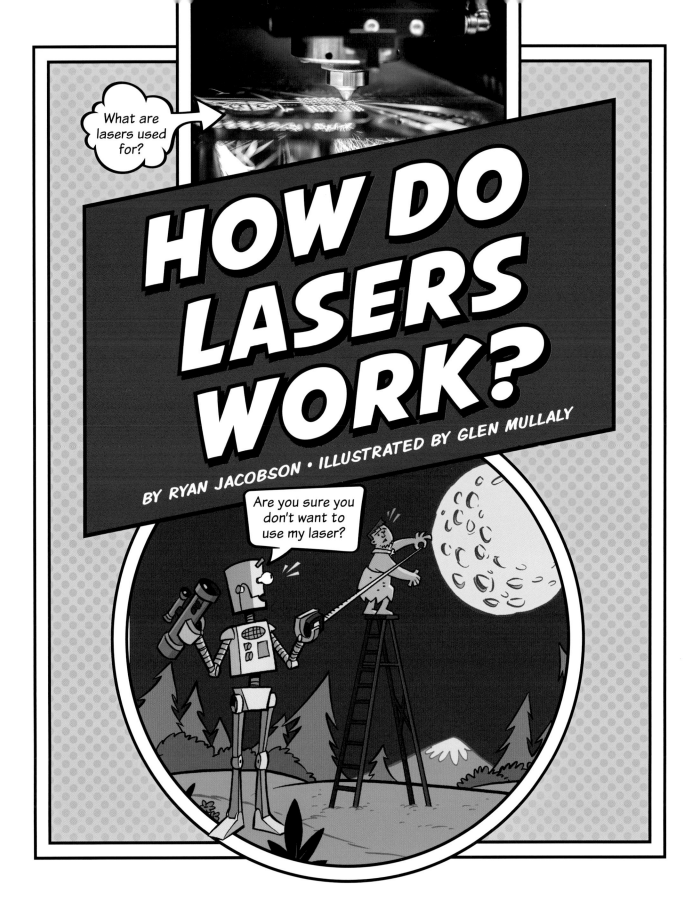

How does this work?

Turn the page to find out!

ABOUT THE AUTHOR

Ryan Jacobson is a successful author and presenter. He has written more than 50 children's books—including picture books, graphic novels, chapter books and choose-your-path books. He has presented at dozens of schools, organizations, and special events. Ryan lives in Minnesota with his wife and two sons.

ABOUT THE ILLUSTRATOR

Glen Mullaly draws neato pictures for kids of all ages from his swanky studio on the west coast of Canada. He lives with his awesomely understanding wife and their spectacularly indifferent cat. Glen loves old books, magazines, and cartoons, and someday wants to illustrate a book on How Monsters Work!

The Child's World®
childsworld.com

Published by The Child's World®
1980 Lookout Drive • Mankato, MN 56003-1705
800-599-READ • www.childsworld.com

Copyright © 2022 by The Child's World®
All rights reserved. No part of this book may be reproduced or utilized in any form or by any means without written permission from the publisher.

ISBN 9781503855953 (Reinforced Library Binding)
ISBN 9781503856028 (Portable Document Format)
ISBN 9781503856264 (Online Multi-user eBook)
LCCN: 2021939378

Photo Credits © Andrey Armyagov/Shutterstock.com: cover, 1, 29; Devteev/Shutterstock.com: 23; DJGUK/Shutterstock.com: 15; Duplass /Shutterstock.com: 27; Edin/iStockphoto.com: 25; Rido/Shutterstock.com: 26

Printed in the United States of America

TABLE OF CONTENTS

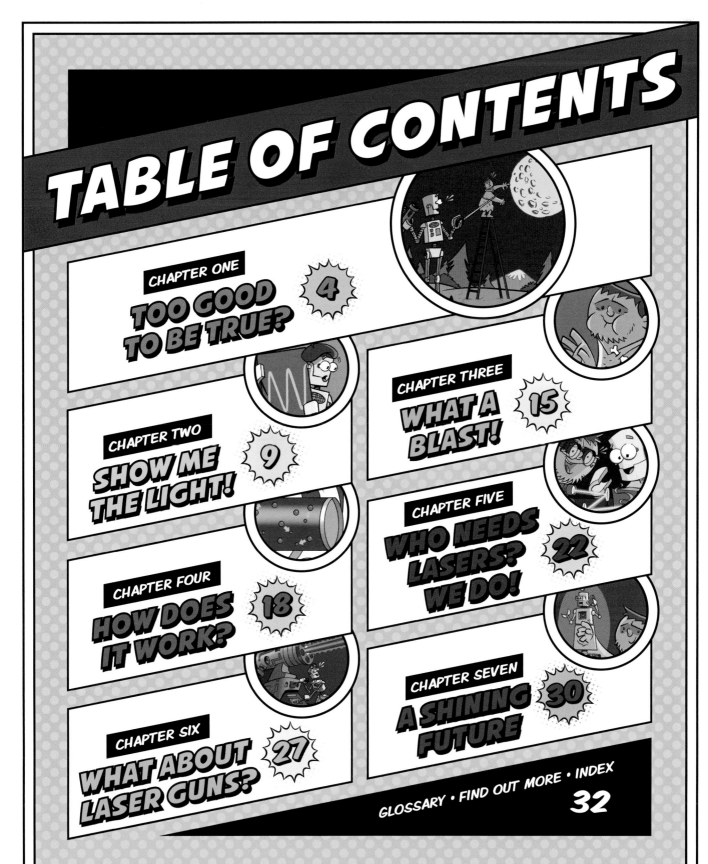

CHAPTER ONE

TOO GOOD TO BE TRUE?

You're on a planet in some far-off solar system. You and your alien friend, Lerp, are in serious trouble. You've just stolen a prized jewel from an army of evil robots. You tried to escape, but you took a wrong turn. Now you're trapped.

Worried? Nah.

You reach into your holster and pull out your very own laser blaster. Those evil robots don't know who they're up against!

Of course, this all sounds like a science fiction story. Alien friends, evil robots, lasers—they aren't real, are they?

Well, we're not so sure about aliens, and evil robots are doubtful. But as for lasers, we use those every day.

Those amazing beams of light help you watch a DVD or check out a book at the library. Have you ever bought something at the grocery store? That probably involved a laser, too.

In fact, lasers have been around for more than 60 years. Let's take a quick look at their history.

Lasers had been around for only 20 years. They were already being used in several ways. Lasers helped doctors during surgery. They allowed scientists to figure out exactly how far away the moon was. Soldiers used them to target their enemies.

100 YEARS AGO

Lasers weren't invented yet. In fact, no one had even thought of them. But in 1917, Albert Einstein came up with the idea that started it all. His idea began with **atoms**, those tiny units of matter. He believed that if you added energy to atoms, you could make them give off light. (And, of course, he was right!)

1,000 YEARS AGO

Lasers? No chance. There wasn't even electricity or light bulbs or toilet paper. People used things like candles to see in the dark.

BACK TO TODAY

Lasers are all around us. We use them to listen to music, play video games—and for so many other things. Who knows what new and different ways we'll use lasers in the future?

WHAT'S IN A WORD?

L LIGHT
A AMPLIFICATION BY
S STIMULATED
E EMISSION OF
R RADIATION

Every letter in the word LASER stands for a different word. But what in the world does that mean?

- **Light amplification** is creating more light from a little light.
- **Stimulate** means to cause something to happen.
- An **emission** is a thing that's made and released from an object.
- **Radiation** is a kind of energy.

Now, let's put it all together:

Light amplification	by	stimulated	emission	of	radiation.
Creating more light	by	causing	the release	of	energy.

So in simple terms, a laser creates a beam of light by causing some of the energy in atoms to be released. Of course, the scientific way of explaining it is better. Otherwise, a laser would be called a cmlcre. Not as catchy, is it?

CHAPTER TWO

SHOW ME THE LIGHT!

To understand lasers, you have to understand light. First, you have to understand that light is a thing— kind of like a book, a chair, and a plate of cookies are all things.

Light is more than just the brightness that fills a room. It's a moving ray that carries energy. And we can look at light in two different ways: either as **waves** or as **particles**.

It's strange but true—light isn't just one way or the other. Scientists find both ways of thinking about light to be useful. Sometimes waves are easier to understand. Sometimes particles make more sense.

Light as Waves

Light is made up of waves, which are basically moving squiggly lines. Imagine dropping a rock into a pond. You can see waves spread across the pond's surface. Light waves act kind of like those water waves. But light can move through air, water, glass, and even empty space!

A shining light lets out way too many waves to count. The waves shoot out every which way: up, down, left, right, you name it. They overlap and cross each other.

This is true even with a flashlight, which tries to aim light in one direction. Imagine shining a flashlight across a dark room. The circle of light on the far wall is bigger than the one coming out. The light has spread out a little.

A RAINBOW OF COLORS

The color of light we see depends on the light's **wavelength**. A wavelength is the distance from the top of one wave to the next. In a rainbow, violet has the shortest wavelength. Yellow has an average wavelength, and red has the longest. We see white light when many different-sized wavelengths are mixed together.

Light as Particles

All things—including you and that plate of cookies—are made up of tiny particles called atoms. Atoms are so small, it takes a super-strong microscope to even see them.

Atoms are always moving. Even the atoms that make up a wall, a rock, and your lazy Uncle Fred move 100 percent of the time. Atoms are full of energy. Sometimes an atom's energy escapes in the form of an even smaller particle. That's called a **photon**. This photon energy is what we see as light.

"Wait a minute." (That's you talking.) "I thought light was waves." Well, yes, that's true. And we're still talking about the same light as before. But now, instead of imagining it as waves, we're imagining it as particles. It's just a different way of thinking about light.

DO THE PHOTON DANCE!

Atoms are cool. They're like little solar systems. The middle of an atom has a nucleus, kind of like the sun. **Electrons** orbit that nucleus like planets. Those electrons never stop moving around the nucleus.

So, electrons orbit a nucleus . . . and the path they travel is also called an orbit. Some orbits—paths—are near the outside of the atom. They are bigger than the orbits closer to the middle. Sometimes, while an atom is wiggling, one of its electrons will move from a large orbit to a smaller one. That's when the atom gives off one photon. Turn on a light bulb, and lots of atoms give off lots of photons.

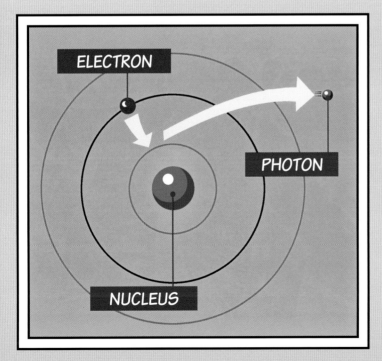

ELECTRON

PHOTON

NUCLEUS

100 KINDS

Everything in the entire universe is made from just about 100 kinds of atoms. So, what's the difference between water, your house, and even your weird next-door neighbor? It all comes down to how the atoms are put together.

CHAPTER THREE
WHAT A BLAST!

A laser creates a perfectly straight beam of light. Here, too, we can look at laser beams as either waves or particles.

Waves

We've already learned that light's waves crisscross and move every which way. Is that also true for laser

This laser is being used to ensure a surface is level.

light? Nope! In a laser, all the waves move together in one direction. The waves are also all the same size. This makes a very tight, straight beam that has only one color, such as red or green.

Particles

Do you remember those tiny atoms that make up everything around us? And how photons escape from atoms to create light? Well, that's an important part of understanding lasers.

A laser contains atoms, which come from a gas, a liquid, or a solid. A laser works by giving these atoms extra energy. The atoms get more and more energy until they have way too much. The atoms need to get rid of their extra energy, so they make and release photons. It's kind of like a balloon that fills up with air until it pops.

TYPES OF LASERS

There are all kinds of lasers made out of all kinds of materials. Here are just a few kinds:

- **Dye laser:** This liquid laser uses a dye that looks like food coloring, but it is very poisonous. This laser can shoot a beam of almost any color.
- **Gas laser:** This common laser is used for cutting and welding. It is also used by doctors for some kinds of surgeries.
- **Semiconductor laser:** You've probably seen this one in action. It is used in medical treatments and to scan barcodes on the things we buy.
- **Solid-state laser:** This was the first kind of laser invented. It is now used to cut metals.

THE LONG AND SHORT OF IT

Lasers come in all sizes. They can be smaller than a penny or bigger than a house. The largest laser in the world is as wide as three football fields!

CHAPTER FOUR

HOW DOES IT WORK?

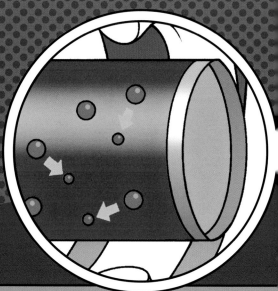

1. Inside the laser, electricity is zapped into the spiral tube. The tube shines bright white for just an instant.

2. The flash of light hits the ruby crystal. This adds energy to the crystal's atoms . . .

POWER SUPPLY

SWITCH

How is a laser beam made? Let's go through the process, step by step. For our example, we'll use the ruby laser: the first laser ever invented.

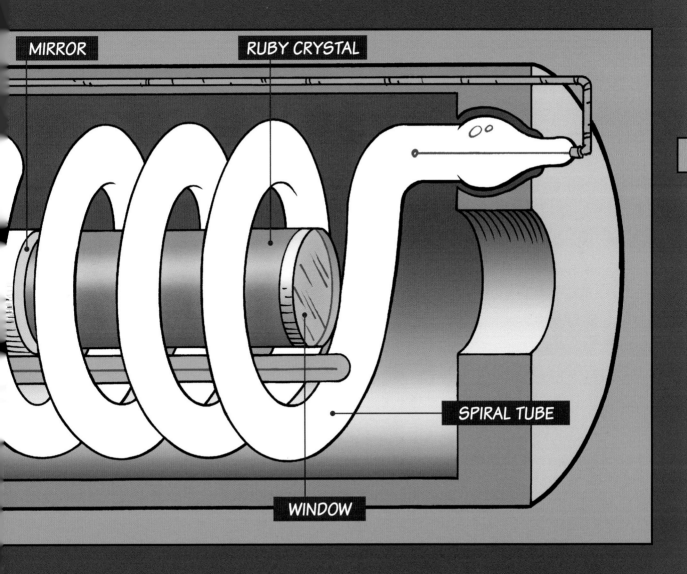

MIRROR

RUBY CRYSTAL

SPIRAL TUBE

WINDOW

3. The atoms with extra energy give off photons. These photons bounce in all directions inside the crystal. They add energy to other atoms, creating even more photons.

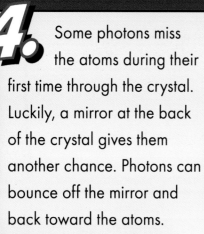

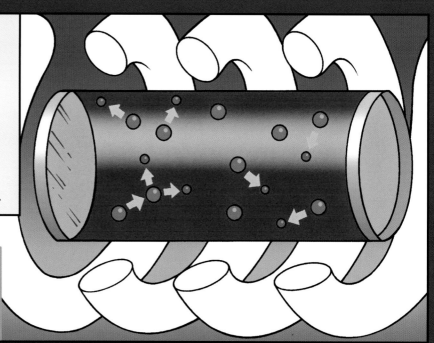

4. Some photons miss the atoms during their first time through the crystal. Luckily, a mirror at the back of the crystal gives them another chance. Photons can bounce off the mirror and back toward the atoms.

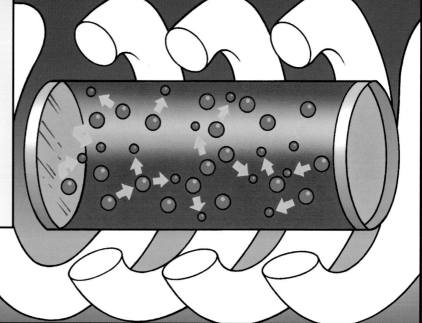

5. A special, glass window at the front of the crystal lets out some photons, making a laser beam. Other photons bounce off the window and back into the crystal. This gives them another chance to add energy to the atoms and make the laser even brighter.

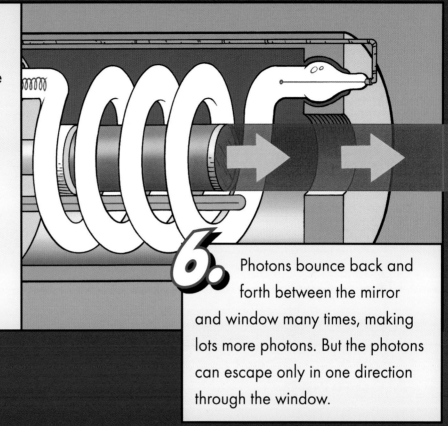

6. Photons bounce back and forth between the mirror and window many times, making lots more photons. But the photons can escape only in one direction through the window.

BLINK AND YOU'LL MISS IT

This sounds like a long process. It can take millions—sometimes trillions—of photons to make a laser beam. But all of it happens in the blink of an eye.

CHAPTER FIVE

WHO NEEDS LASERS? WE DO!

There are so many ways to use lasers. Here are just a few common ways:

Measuring

Because lasers make a perfectly straight line, they're perfect for measuring. Scientists use lasers to measure very short distances—way too small for a ruler. But lasers also come in handy for very long distances, too. In fact, scientists have used laser light to figure out exactly how far the moon is from Earth!

But wait. How can we measure distance with light?

Well, it helps to know that light always travels at the same speed: 186,287 miles (299,800 km) per second. In kid terms, that's "really, really, really fast."

It also helps to know that there's a handy math formula that goes: distance = speed x time. Let's say your best friend is walking from his house to your house. You know how

These scientists in Switzerland are using a laser to measure things in space.

fast he's walking. (That's the speed part.) You know how long it takes him to do the whole walk. (That's the time part.) Multiply those two numbers, and you can find the distance between your houses.

So, in this case, the laser beam is like your friend. It provides the speed. Next, scientists need a time. So, they clock how long it takes a laser beam to hit an object. They multiply that time by the speed of light—186,287 miles per second. Their answer is the total distance.

MOON MATH

The distance to the moon changes slightly depending on where the moon is in its orbit around Earth. At one point, though, it takes a laser beam exactly 1.2829 seconds to hit the moon. And 1.2829 x 186,287 = 238,987. So we know that the moon is 238,987 miles from Earth.

CDs, DVDs and Video Games

Do you like music, movies, or games? (Who doesn't?) Then you should love lasers! Lasers are used to record and play back all of your favorite kinds of entertainment disks, from *Mummy Warriors 5* to *Attack of the Slime Monster.*

Whether it's a song or a movie scene, each starts as digital data stored on a computer. A tiny laser beam cuts this data onto the bottom of a disk. Look closely at the bottom of a DVD or video game disk (or a CD, if you or your parents can find one around). Can you believe it's covered with little bumps and grooves? It is! And they're all made by lasers.

A disk usually gets put into a player with the "bumpy" side down. The player spins the disk very fast, while a low-powered laser shoots it. The laser hits the bumps and grooves. It reflects back as a special signal. The player changes this signal into electricity and plays it for you to see or hear.

So the next time you're beating your best friend in *Caveman vs. Robot*, say a special thanks to lasers.

A laser reading a DVD

Barcodes

Take a quick look at the back of this book. Did you see the little white box full of thick and thin black lines? This is called a barcode. Most things we buy have one.

How does a barcode work? First, a special laser called a scanner passes its light over a barcode. The light reflects off the barcode and signals a computer at the store. The signal tells the computer to find information about the item, such as a book title and its price. The computer sends that information to wherever it's needed—like a cash register where you're standing.

Shipping companies use barcodes to keep track of where everything is going.

And how does this help you? Well, unless you really enjoy standing in line, you should be happy. Scanners make paying for groceries and whatever else your parents might buy go much quicker.

CHAPTER SIX

WHAT ABOUT LASER GUNS?

All right . . . all right . . . this is all very interesting.
But you want to get back to laser guns, don't you? Are
they real? Do laser weapons really exist? You might be
surprised to know the answer is yes—but probably not
in the way you think.

TIME LINE

1917	**1954**	**1960**	**1961**
Albert Einstein comes up with the idea that atoms can be made to give off light.	Three American scientists build a "maser." It makes a beam of microwave rays instead of light.	The world's first laser beam is created.	A New York doctor uses a laser during eye surgery.

Time line continued

Lasers were first used by the military almost 40 years ago. In 1972, soldiers fighting in the Vietnam War shone laser lights at enemy targets. The lasers were signals to missiles, telling them what to blow up.

1969
A laser helps measure the exact distance from Earth to the moon.

1972
Soldiers use lasers to target enemies during the Vietnam War.

1978
The US Navy shoots down a missile with a laser.

1980
CDs are introduced.

1982
Billy Joel's 52nd Street becomes the first album released on CD.

Time line continued

A few years later, during a test, scientists destroyed a missile with a laser beam. Cool, huh? That led to a US military program that everyone called Star Wars. The plan was to launch lasers (attached to satellites) into outer space. The lasers would orbit Earth.

More than 3,000 satellites orbit, or circle, Earth.

If an enemy fired a missile at the United States, the Star Wars lasers would shoot it down.

The plan didn't work, though. Star Wars was dropped because it cost a lot of money. Plus, the lasers weren't always able to destroy the missiles. But it's not the end of the story. The United States is still trying to figure out the best way to use lasers as weapons.

1983	1987	1993	2003	TODAY
The United States begins its Star Wars program.	Video CDs are created.	The Star Wars program is dropped.	The world's first Blu-Ray players become available in Japan.	Lasers are used everywhere, in nearly all industries worldwide.

CHAPTER SEVEN
A SHINING FUTURE

Lasers have been around for only 60 years, and we've already found hundreds of uses for them. Who can guess what the next 100 years will bring? Some experts think lasers will help make inventions like these part of everyday life:

- Hologram movies: We will be able to watch movies in 3-D, without the glasses.
- Telephone projector: When you videocall with someone, their image will hang in the air like a hologram.
- Energy: Lasers will become a source for unlimited energy—no more stopping at the gas station!

How about you? What ideas do you have for future lasers? After all, it seems that if someone can dream it up, lasers will probably be able to do it!

JUST THE RIGHT AMOUNT

One reason lasers have so many uses is that they're packed with different amounts of power. Some laser beams are so hot and strong that they can cut through steel. Others are very weak and couldn't even cut through your homework!

GLOSSARY

atom (AT-um): An atom is a tiny unit of matter. Atoms create light by giving off photons.

electron (ih-LEK-tron): An electron is the part of an atom that orbits the center, or nucleus. When an electron moves from a bigger orbit to a smaller orbit, it gives off a photon.

particle (PAR-tuh-kuhl): A particle is a tiny bit of something. Light can be thought of as particles.

photon (FOH-ton): A photon is a small particle of energy released by an atom. Scientists think of light as photons.

wave (WAYV): A wave can be thought of as a squiggly line of moving energy. Scientists think of light as waves.

wavelength (WAYV-lehngkth): A wavelength is the distance from the top of one wave to the top of the next one. A light's wavelength determines its color.

Visit our Web site for links about how lasers work: childsworld.com/links

Note to Parents, Teachers, and Librarians: We routinely verify our Web links to make sure they are safe and active sites. So encourage your readers to check them out!

INDEX